The Festival

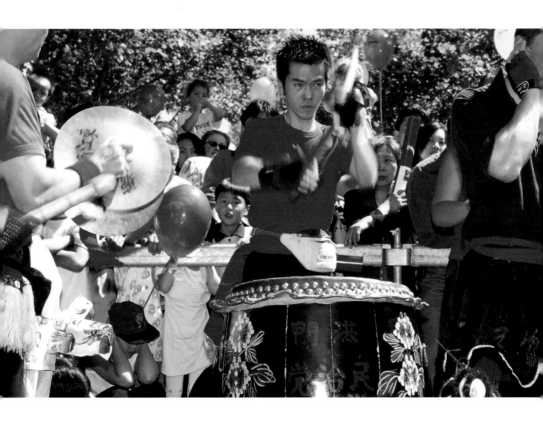

Wil Spencer

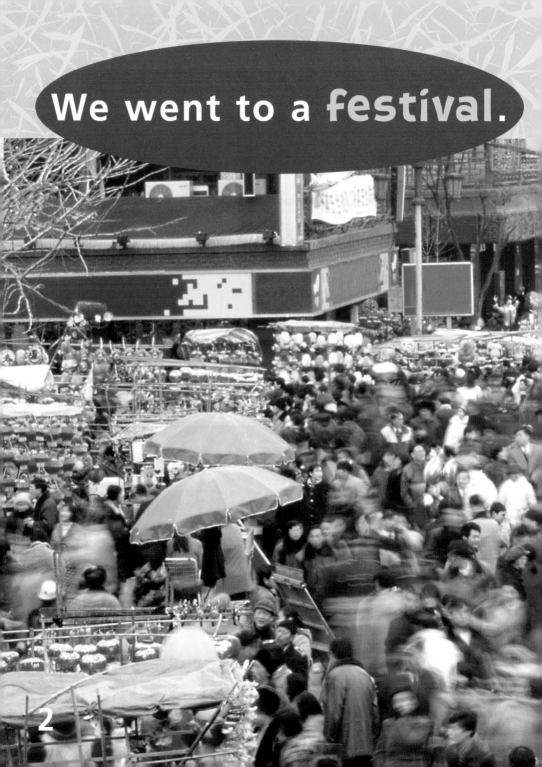

We went to a festival.

2

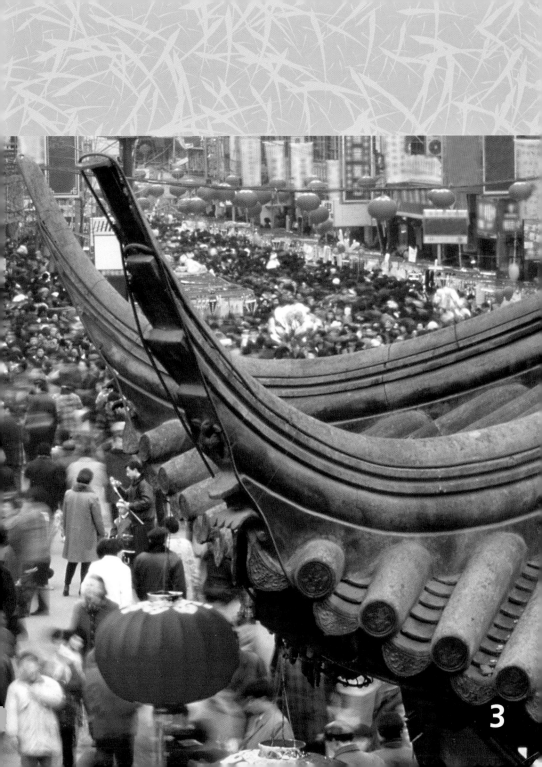

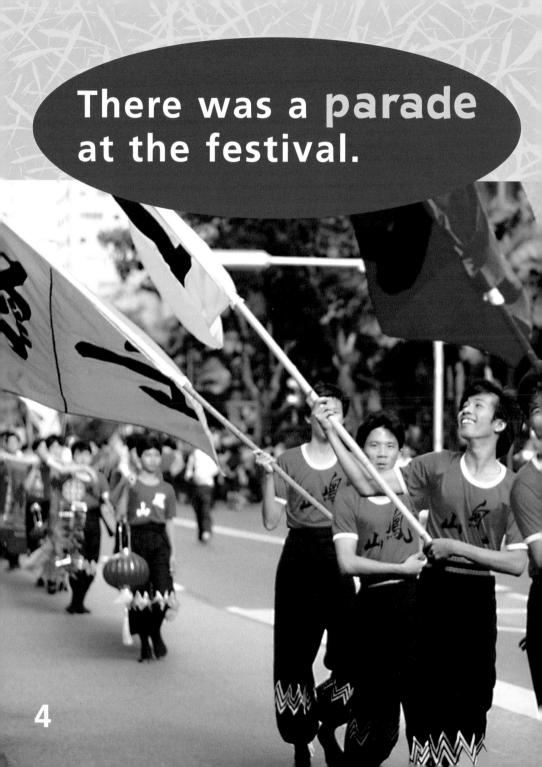

There was a parade
at the festival.

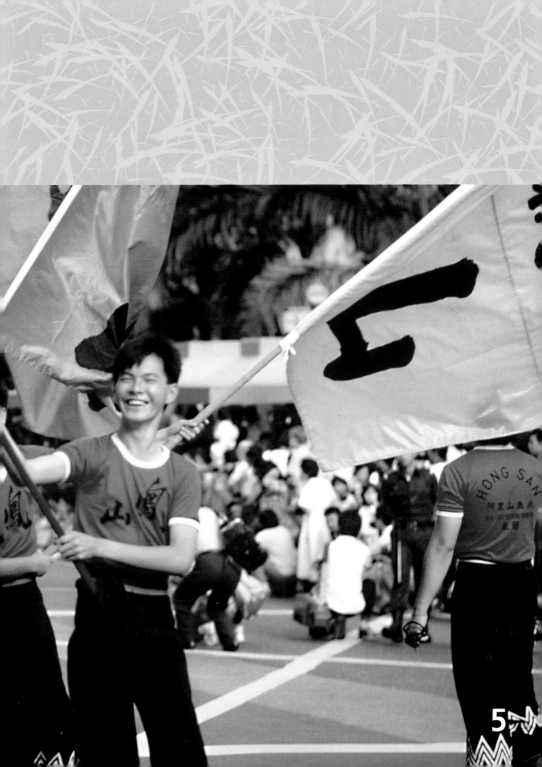

5

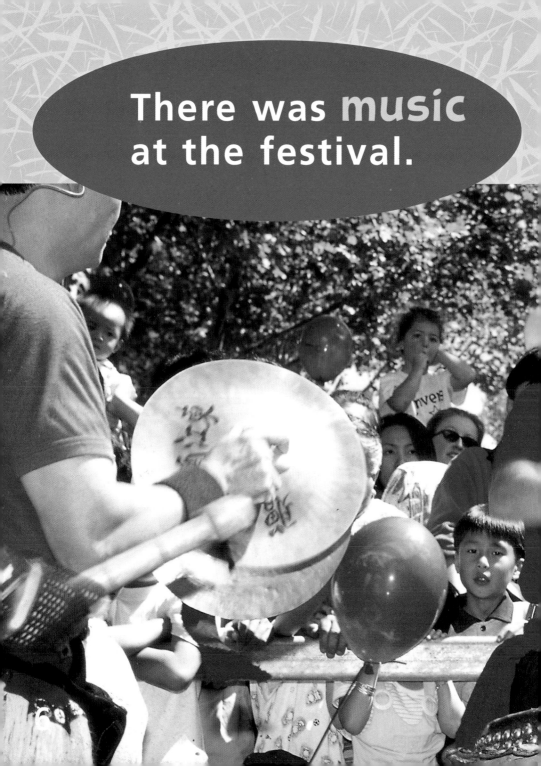

There was **music** at the festival.

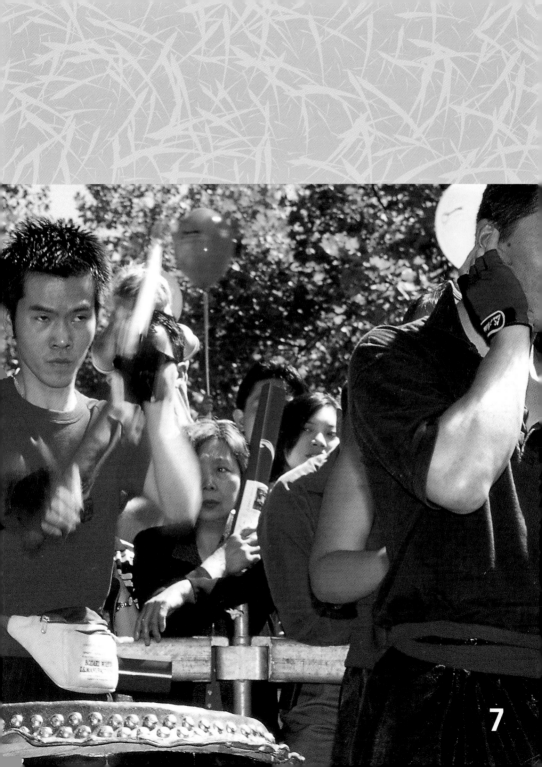

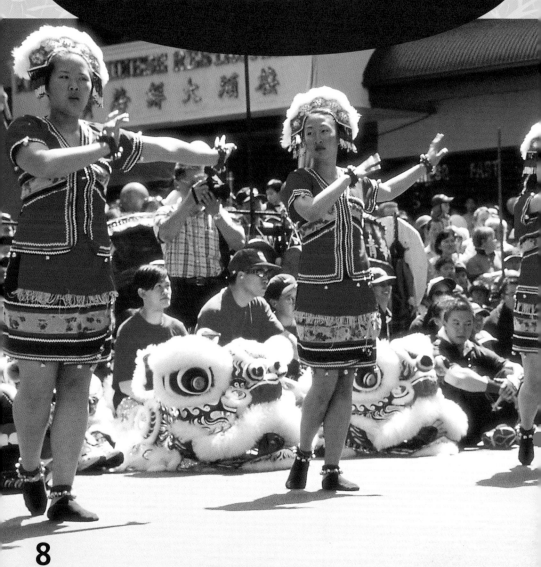

There was dancing at the festival.

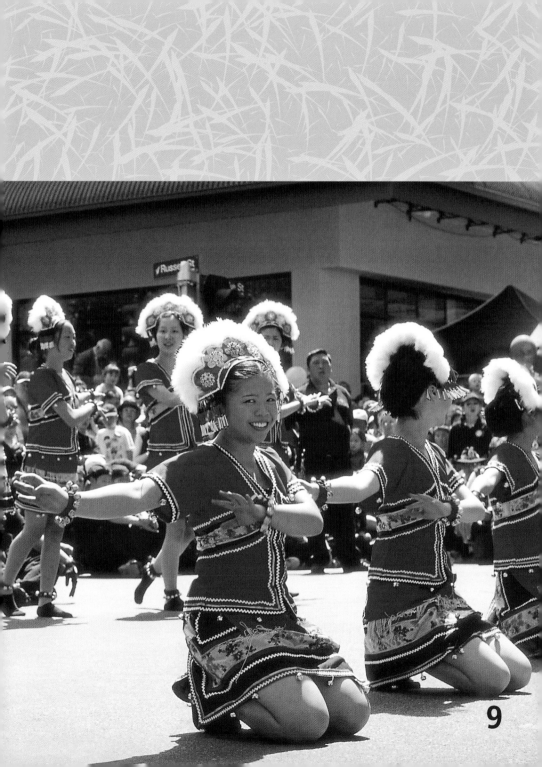

9

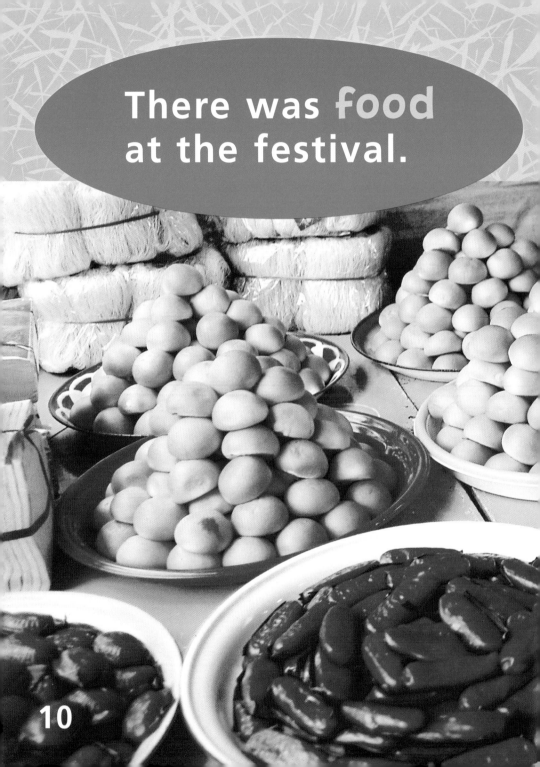

There was food
at the festival.

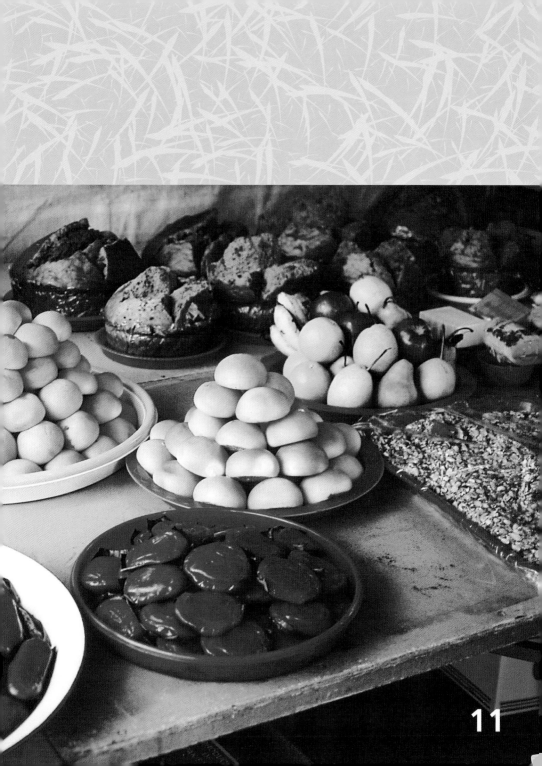

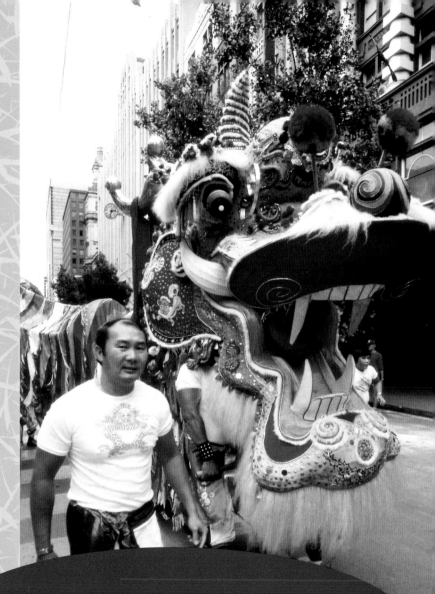

There was a **dragon** at the festival.